Our F
Vacation

by Rafael Melo
illustrated by Bob Masheris

HOUGHTON MIFFLIN BOSTON

Printed in China

ISBN-13: 978-0-547-02013-6
ISBN-10: 0-547-02013-9

14 15 16 17 0940 19 18 17 16
4500569761

We like to fish.

We like to swim.

We like to climb.

We like to cook.

We like to sleep.

Responding

TARGET SKILL **Story Structure**

Where does this story take place? Who are the characters? Tell what happens in the story. Make a chart.

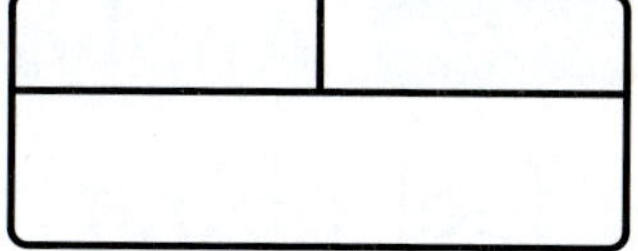

Talk About It

Text to Self Have you ever gone on a trip with your family? Draw a picture of the trip. Tell about your picture.

good	said

TARGET SKILL **Story Structure**

Tell the setting, characters, and events in a story.

TARGET STRATEGY **Analyze/Evaluate**

Tell how you feel about the text, and why.

GENRE **Fiction** is a story that is made up.